Life Interrupted

A Mother's Grief Journey
after The Loss of Her Daughter

KATRINA FISHER-GETER

Foreword by Rev. Dr. Candace Cole-Kelly

Life Interrupted: A Mother's Grief Journey After the Loss of Her Daughter
by Katrina Fisher-Geter

Copyright © 2023 Katrina Fisher-Geter
All rights reserved.
Printed and bound in the United States of America

Published by Cole Publishing
No reproduction of any part of this format, contents or artistic contributions
can be made without written permission from the author.

Library of Congress
Cataloging-in-Publication Data

ISBN: 979-8-9885825-3-3

Cole Publishing
4067 Hardwick Street #282
Lakewood, CA 90712
Email: ccpprod@aol.com

Book Cover Design by Covenant Images
This cover has been designed using assets from Freepik.com
For Book Orders:
Contact us at Cole Publishing Company

Cole Publishing

CONTENTS

DEDICATION

This book is dedicated to my family and my pastor/spiritual father Dr. Angelo Conway, who often told his congregation that we all have a book in us. Thus, here is my book.

This book is also dedicated to those that have faced tragedies in their lives and decide to get up each day and keep going through the hurt and the pain.

As I share my story, I pray it blesses someone and helps them to deal with the interruption life has thrown their way through tragedies. I encourage them to keep going knowing that you can make it through one day at a time. In times of trouble know that God promises to always be by our side and to never leave us.

"God is our refuge and strength, A very present help in trouble."

PSALM 46:1

SPECIAL THANKS AND ACKNOWLEDGEMENTS

This could not have happened without God ordained support and prayers. I first thank my Savior and Lord, Jesus Christ for His Strength! I thank my beloved husband and one flesh Mr. Darryle Geter. You have been the wind beneath my wings and you have blessed me with unconditional love, patience, encouragement and prayer. I love you!!! To my heroic son, Mr. Brandon Fisher-Geter, you are my rock also! You are the greatest son a mother could ever have. Always know how proud and thankful I am of you. to my Pastor and Spiritual Covering, Bishop Conway and First Lady. Your support and presence during the most darkest time of my life cannot be captured with mere words. I can't say thank you and my church family enough for your prayers and support. To Ms. Felicia Jackson, please know that your presence in my life during this time has been amazing and I so appreciate you from the bottom of my heart. To my entire family, thank you for the foundation you built for me and the example you displayed of your love, kindness, prayers and support. I love you with my life!

To my beloved Mentor, Rev. Dr. Candace Cole-Kelly, and my publisher: God sent you all the way to Tennessee from California just for me. He showed me how much he loved me by letting our paths cross for Kingdom Purposes. I thank you for your encouragement, empowerment, godly example, and friendship. You gently held space for me and birthed through me this beautiful memoir "Life Interrupted". Thank you over and over again for being that gentle midwife!

FOREWORD

By Rev. Dr. Candace Cole-Kelly

Gift, Grit and Glory of Life

We live with goals, aspirations, hopes, dreams, and yet there are no solid guarantees that we will reach all of them. A wise person once said, "People living their life and coming to its end are there for all of us to see. We think we know about life and how to live it, how to love and how to be bereft, because these things are ubiquitous and right before our eyes. Those who take care of others—for example, counselors, psychologists, chaplains, pastors, nurses, and physicians—are especially privileged to be a part of the lives of others and to have the opportunity to gain understanding of sickness, suffering, troubles and interruptions."

The reality is, however, that many people do not learn well from others due to the barrier of being fully present. Even those who by profession should know the most about life and death or love and grief often seem lacking in this regard. It leaves one asking, "Why do people see but not see, listen but not hear?" The famous, Goethe said that one sees what one knows, or, turned around, what you already know tells you what you are seeing and tells you what the words you are hearing mean." So, the gift, grit and glory of life can be obscure in the enterprise of holding on so close to the love you once beheld. Katrina Fisher-Geter's vulnerability seeks to explore this paradoxical journey of grief with no apologies and sufficient grace. She shares candidly that there are no cookie cutter venues to processing, deep grief that suddenly interrupts your life with no notice, but with one moment at a time, one hour at a time, one breath at a time, you can make it through! The only way out is through! This book is the tell all from, a mother's wounded heart grappling at life as it slips away one morning from her very presence. She reminds her readers that her Lord and Savior whispered to her, "we may grieve, but not as those who have no hope." A powerfully healing book for all to read.

INTRODUCTION

I penned the words to this life transforming book to simply share my journey of the hills, the valleys, and the interruptions that can take your breath away leaving you almost lifeless.

My learnings at the time of this writing are profound. I learned no matter the depth of despair and the height of obscurity and confusion, you can be found by God who is able to keep you from self-destruction.

The journey which led you to pick up this book is one of providence. It is my hope and prayer that it will be a source of strength and affirmation. Finally, I truly want you to know that you can make it through any of life's untimely interruptions. By no means is it an easy task, just know that it is possible to make it through with the presence of God's amazing Grace.

"Nay, in all these things we are more than conquerors through him that loves us."

Romans 8:37

CHAPTER ONE

Shattered to Pieces

Life can be dauntingly obscure and tragically unpredictable. That is how I will describe my existence during the first and hopefully, the only Pandemic I will live through.

Then the economic climate was devastated as companies and organizations had to shut down their businesses due to the pandemic which cut off their financial resources. Tragedy, after tragedy emerged in the American landscape. For the first time in our history, everyone was experiencing just about the same devastation of uncertainty.

Politically, Economically, Spiritually and Psychologically, we were on edge. We were crushed as a people, but nothing could prepare me for what came next. My life was truly interrupted.

It was August 8, 2021, at 4:20p.m. That Sunday afternoon is as clear in my mind as if it was today. I am convinced that there are events that you will never be able to erase from your soul.

I remember being on my 9th day of COVID. It was my son and daughter's 5th day of having Covid. My son's symptoms were very light, and he reported only having a slight headache for a couple of days and then he was fine. But my daughter on the other hand seemed to be fine with a cough so we thought. Even though she was upbeat she coughed throughout that Saturday night quite a bit, but she was on the telephone laughing and talking with her friends.

I could hear her deep into the night still coughing, into the wee wee hours of the morning, coughing.

I was still weak with hardly any strength or energy. I felt something was wrong in my spirit. I mustered up enough strength to yell and ask my daughter if she was alright, because I of all the coughing, "yes mom, I'm okay."

"Did you take your cough medicine?" I asked.

She yells back, "Yes, I'm fine mom."

She was upbeat and in good spirits, so I thought no more about it. I was thankful she was having fun, even thou that cough would not let her go. As a parent, it feels powerless to not be able to help heal your children, no matter how old they are. A mother never wants to see their child in pain or discomfort. God made us that way; I suppose because He is that way too.

The following morning, I was still slightly concerned. I had one consolation and that was that she slept all night. I could hear her snoring from the other room, so I know she got some good rest, finally.

Later that day, (Sunday morning August 8th) I slowly walked into her room. I began to pray over her and kind of moved her covers down a bit as I was praying over her body for God to heal her.

I heard her say, "ma," as she quickly pulled her covers back up to her neck. I chucked,

"I'm sorry baby." I didn't know that brief humorous encounter would be the last words we would utter to each other and that would be our last interaction I would ever have with my 23-year-old daughter.

I left her room still chuckling a bit (from me pulling down her covers accidentally and her snatching them up to her neck as quickly as she did) after I finished praying for her.

"Behold children are a heritage and gift from the Lord,
The fruit of the womb a reward."

PSALM 127:3

Strength was returning to my body, little by little. I was happy to call my mother to give her an update on all of us, my son, daughter as well as myself. I shared with my mother that I was a little worried that my daughter coughed off and on throughout the night, but she seemed to be alright now because she was sleeping. I could even hear her in my room snoring, so I was relieved that she had stopped coughing and was getting some rest.

Our appetites began to return to us later that evening. I couldn't believe no one had eaten yet, and it was well into the evening a little past 4'oclock. In the living room my son, my husband and I kept going back and forth about what we wanted to.

So, my husband asked our son to go into his sister's room to see if she was hungry and what she wanted to eat. I had already dialed the number to the restaurant and proceeded to give the person on the other end part of our food order already while I was waiting for my daughter to tell my son what she wanted to eat.

"Mom, dad, y'all might want to get in here fast," my son comely projected from my daughter's room.

And just like that our life was interrupted and took an unexpected turn that no one saw coming of even thought would happen on that particular day.

Even though he said it calmly we knew there was urgency needed on our part. He continued to speak to us,

"Usually when I touch her face while she is sleeping, she hits my hand. She did not hit my hand this time and tell me to stop, something is wrong!"

My husband ran into her room and yelled my name, "Trina! You might want to get in here now!" I tell the person on the phone "I will call you back."

I jumped up as fast as I could from sitting on the edge of the bed on the phone ordering food. I am still relatively weak from having had COVID.

I am moving as fast as my body would allow me to move. I jumped into some clothes and ran into my daughter's room as fast as I could. I saw her, I saw her body, I called out her name and shook her, nothing, no response from her at all. My husband, my son was standing in shock and disbelief.

At this point I called 911! I will never forget making that call as long as I live. While I was on the phone with the 911 operator, I began to touch my daughter's head, it was still warm! "She is not breathing", She has COVID."

"Mam, where is your daughter?"
"She's in her bed."

The operator calmly instructed me to "move her to the floor. My husband and I moved her to the floor. I immediately started to administer CPR to her per the operators' instructions.

My son and husband go outside. It's just me and her alone in that room. My baby is not responding. My heart beating a thousand beats a second it feels like. I continue to administer CPR until the paramedics arrives.

The whole entire time I'm doing CPR on her I was so weak, temperature rising, feeling hot and so exhausted as if I myself was about to pass out but I knew I had to keep going.

My child's life was in my hands I thought at that very moment. I could not stop. Although, I felt in my heart of hearts that she was already gone, I had to keep going and could not and would not give up on my child. I kept going all the while trying to keep it together. I remember thinking in my head, I cannot break now as I felt her body was still warm, so I had a glimpse of hope I thought, because she was not ice cold.

Then as I rose up to look at her beautiful face, a small trickle of saliva ran out of the corner of the right side of her mouth. I then saw she had already soiled her bed. This couldn't be happening, I felt with my heart in my throat.

Weak and weary, I continue to administer CPR on her having more urgency each time more than the last time as I did chest compresses. I kept telling myself, I must try, I cannot stop, I am her mother, and this is my child! That thought kept replaying in my head over and over at that moment, I kept going as I wiped the warm trickle of saliva off the corner of her mouth with my hand as I continued to do CPR. It seemed like forever until the paramedics finally arrived.

"Mam', we got it from here, mam, we got it now," the soft spoken EMT said as he gently nudges me to the right.

Which seemed like it took them forever to arrive, I was so hot, tired, and weak but I could not and did not stop until the paramedics said it was ok to stop even though they had arrived and took over.

After the paramedics took over, my body felt as though I was about to drop to the floor at that very moment.

Somehow, I gained enough strength to walk across the hall to my bedroom and fell to my knees and did the only thing I knew how to do in times of trouble which was to kneel down and pray to my God and Father.

"God, I need your strength! I need your Peace, I need Your, strength, God. Please give me your Strength. God, Oh, God, Oh God, please Strengthen me with Your Peace!"

Why I prayed for only those two things, I cannot say. I was so weak; I can only surmise that is what the Holy Spirit was praying through me.

The paramedics came to my side to ask me important questions about my daughter. He had his pen and notepad ready. I had to give him her full name, her social security number, among other things. For the life of me, I could not give him one answer to any of his questions in that very moment. I found myself holding my head trying to think but could not. "I'm so sorry sir, I can't think, I'm so sorry." I kept telling the paramedic. I wanted to remember her birthday, her social security and anything he asked me, but my mind and my brain just could not bring the information to me. I was in shock! I was disoriented and couldn't make sense of much.

I kept apologizing to him because I had no answers and he kept saying, "It's okay mam, it's really okay, we understand." My emotions were mixed, "how could I not remember," I wondered to myself. Frustration was sitting in. It felt like I was in two worlds all at the same time.

I went outside pacing the grounds, until my family, neighbors and friends rallied around me. EMT's finally came out with defeat and regret written all over their demeanors. "We are sorry mam', we are so sorry to tell you we did all that we could do, and our efforts were not..." the young man was emotional himself.

"Blessed are they that mourn: for they shall be comforted."

Matthew 5:4

Life Interrupted Reflection Questions

1. Describe a life interruption.

2. Where were you?

3. What was said?

4. Who delivered the news?

5. How did you handle it?

6. What was helpful?

7. What was hurtful?

8. What would you have liked to be different?

9. Did you feel alone?

10. Did you feel supported?

CHAPTER 2

Living In Grief

The second reason I was compelled to write this part of my journey is to be a source of strength and support to grieving individuals.

This chapter is entitled "Living in Grief" because I have discovered, grief is simply that after you lose someone so close to you, you then must live in it. There is no way of getting around it, under it or over it. You have to live with it before you can heal from it.

I had to live with the loss of my only daughter, my baby girl and my princess. I lost her and I had to accept that reality at some point on this journey as I kept gasping to save her life that was not coming back to me. I have to live into my grief.

Grief is many things to many people. For me, grief is the emotional state, the feeling you feel after one's death. You are right there living in what is now your newness in life.

I learned through this process that it is also helpful to know the difference between grief and grieving in order to be able to heal properly.

My experience with grief is that raw emotion that you feel that can and will come over you at any given time or place.

As for grieving, in my own experience it is the process that you will go through as you realize that your loved one is no longer here and is gone forever, and that process (grieving) you will have to carry as long as you live.

Living in grief is one of the hardest things I have ever had to endure. It is like a sadness that seems like it will never go away and sometimes it feels as though it is a heavy load but other days it feels like it is a lite load to carry. It can also be described for me as a battle of many feelings fighting against one another that you must overcome somehow someway.

My grieving process drew me to my prayer closest more than I have than I had ever prayed in my entire life.

Right after my daughter passed, we stayed at a hotel that night. The entire ride to the hotel was like riding in a fog of shock and disbelief. We rode in complete silence. I don't think any of us really slept that night. I was just shattered into pieces. I did not know what to think or how to feel. I just knew our lives had just been interrupted and what we once knew was no more.

The next day we left the hotel and headed home. We drove home just the way we drove to the hotel, mostly in silence it was still like it was not really real in my head because it did not seem real even though she was gone and I knew it, but it still seemed unreal to me.

Then I noticed something undeniable. There was a stillness in and a really strange calmness in the air like, the kind that happens right before a big storm. The feeling was so surreal. We did not talk about it at all at that moment. I think we (my son, husband, and myself) were trying to grasp what had happened the previous day and process the thought of her really being gone forever. Death is so final! No grey areas, its done!

We arrived home and even though I had not planned or thought about it, I knew what I had to do in that moment for me.

Even though it may seem strange to some I went straight to her room and began to clean it up and clear out all her belongings. Something inside of me needed everything gone that was associated with her. Was it my need to take away all hope of her coming back? Was it too painful to have anything that reminded me of her? Was it extreme grief? There are no right or wrong answers to those questions. There are no cookie cutter ways to grieve!

I often hear others say it took them a while to go into a loved one's room after they pass away, but for me there was a need of urgency for me that I cannot explain, that I felt that I had to do it at that very moment, or I would not be able to do it later. My sisters came over, and they asked me gently "are you sure you want to clean her room out?" I appreciated their love and their courage to gently ask.

For me grief is feeling numb, empty, confused, sad, vulnerable, up down, and having many questions and just going through whatever motion you are feeling at that very moment. There is no order to grief is what I am saying. It doesn't present in nice methodical patterns because I am a witness that all emotions can converge on you all at once sometimes.

Let others love you...

A word of advice to you is when you are living in grief allow people to love you and to love on you as they desire to be there for you. The community gets smaller during seasons of grief because everyone cannot journey with you. No judgement toward them, it's just a unique terrain that everyone cannot travel.

Your grief will tell you not to be a bother and not bring the world down with your loss. Those that want to walk in your grief with you know what a sacred privilege it is to do so because everyone cannot do it. This notion is countercultural for me. I am not naturally comfortable with others having to be there for me.

In times past, I walked through my storms alone, but this loss was so different than any tragedy I had ever faced. I did not resist any support.

Looking back, I can say that I am glad I opened my heart to leaning on others at that time in my life because God knew how much I needed each person that He sent my way.

Grief can be a very humbling experience. When you have an outpour of love and support you will not even notice it because you are consumed with so many different emotions.

It's okay to not be okay…

My heart was so grateful for the loving people that were there for me and my family. I was flooded with so much gratitude. I now know that you cannot do everything by yourself, and I learned that it is ok to not be ok all the time and lean on others in your time of need.

I was blessed enough to have help from my friends and family in making the call to the funeral home, helping plan for the homegoing service, obituaries, errands, repass etc. I am and will be forever grateful for those connected to my daughter and my family.

My beloved daughter passed on a Sunday, and we had her funeral service on that following Saturday.

Our plan was to have her cremated and put her ashes in a beautiful urn. Regrettably, due to COVID, the crematorium was backed up from so many deaths during Covid. So, we had to proceed with her service with an empty urn.

To make matters more challenging because we were in a pandemic there were many friends and community who could not attend the service, which was mainly made up of family and a few close friends. We did a live streaming on Facebook for those that could not attend the service. We got through her funeral service, which was beautiful and simple, just the way she would have wanted it.

Life Interrupted Reflection Questions

1. Describe a loss that you have had. (It could be a loss of a person, pet, job, house, relationship, etc.)

2. How have you grieved this loss?

3. How have you obtained support for yourself, i.e., therapy, prayer, support group, journalling.

4. Where are you on your healing journey?

— KATRINA FISHER-GETER —

CHAPTER 3

The Despair of Delays

Another challenging time followed the end of the funeral service. This is when all the relatives and friends leave and go back to their normal lives. Their absence was as sudden as the passing of my daughter. One moment everyone was there and the next everyone was gone. The visits stopped, the phone calls ceased, the texts started to get fewer and fewer each passing day.

When a community converges and rallies around you day in and day out, you feel a human cushion that buffets the days, hours, and minutes for you. When that leaves, it can be overwhelming and scary. Thoughts of how life will be after the funeral? Anxieties of the countdown to the funeral day and so on. Then it all stops and comes to a head.

Now, don't get me wrong, two years later I still had calls, texts, and those who sent me encouraging and uplifting messages with scriptures, and for that I remain thankful. What is very clear to me is that people typically don't know that grief doesn't have an expiration date.

Grief Hanging in the Balance

The inability to obtain my daughter's ashes added another layer of complicated grief for our family. My mind was in turmoil and confusion. Every day, I would call and call, and still get the same answer "we are so sorry we are so behind". It was equally hard for me to think of my child lying in what I thought of as a cold freezer drawer. I was totally out of control of the situation. I had no authority, no choices or influence. I was powerless! Grief will leave you powerless on this journey with variables that you cannot manage or alter.

After the funeral, was supposed to be the time that I should be moving toward healing putting things to rest, but the absence of her ashes felt like my grief was hanging in the balance. I went through a lot of emotions because of it, i.e., anger, resentment, regrets, guilt, and you name it, I felt it. It was almost a month later when I got the call that I could come pick up her ashes.

I felt an immediate relief and just cried and cried after hanging up the phone. It felt like a weight had been lifted off my shoulder. I picked up her ashes and felt relieved and cried as we drove further and further away from the funeral home with a sigh of relief.

That night I decided to write my baby a letter.

Letter to My Daughter, Bri

Dear Bri,

I have so much to talk about and say to you that I will not be able to say everything that I have to say but, here is some and I'll meet you in my dreams. I wish I could talk to you one last time face to face, and hear your little squeaky, high-pitched voice but you are not here, so I'm writing this letter to you instead one year to the day you departed this place called earth. I never imagined in a million years that you would be gone from this earth at the tender age of 23 without so much as a warning or a goodbye. But I see God had other plans for you and us. There is a big part of our hearts missing (You). Even though I was not a perfect mom I pray that I was the best mother I could have been to you, I did as best as I knew how because there are certainly no redos in this thing call parenting or even life. So, I honestly hope I was what you needed at the time I was blessed enough to be your mother. I wish you were here right now, and I could say these words to you. We had and have so many good and funny memories that I often think of and smile throughout my day and it brings a smile upon my face sometimes and that gets me through that moment or even my day, I can only hope the mistakes I made as your mother was forgiven. You were a wonderful daughter. You had the biggest personality but an even bigger heart. You had the biggest and brightest smile also. You had a presence about yourself that only you carried. You were a great big sister to your brother who misses you even more than I can ever speak of. You were loving, kind, and so gentle. You never gave us any trouble. You were not perfect, but you were perfect for us.

Since you have been gone it's been really hard for everyone you left behind. We don't often speak of it, but we all share and feel an unspoken sadness and each other's pain without saying it out loud. I can say your passing brought two of your favorite cousins together again and your siblings reach out a lot more. You had a different relationship with each one of us and we deal with it differently. All birthdays and holidays are not the same since you left, there is truly a sadness there as well, but we manage to get through it as best as we can by loving on each other in living in the moment as best as we know how. Two of your birthdays have come and gone without you being here. We wear red, your favorite color in remembrance of you. It is so hard for me like a few months before your Birthday and your death date as well. It now seems as if we are just pushing through at the moment trying to survive. Somehow, we all pull ourselves together to get through even though our hearts are heavy and filled with grief and sadness.

I feel like a part of my heart was taken when you left us, and I will never get it back but will have to learn to live without that crucial piece. We miss you so very much and will get through by the Grace of God. I have heard that there is purpose in pain still trying to figure that one out though. I feel as if there is an enormous purpose for the pain I have as your mother. So hopefully that part will be revealed in due time.

I pray a lot and I mean a lot more than I have ever prayed in my life. I know that it is God that is keeping me and allows me to make it each day. I go down but I do not stay there. Prayer is all I know to do, and it gets me through every second, minute, and hour of the day as it brings peace and calmness to me that keeps me going. I have also learned to let myself grieve and feel every single emotion I need to feel when I need to feel it at any given moment. I believe it helps me in my healing process as well.

We often talk about some of the things you said or would do or say if you were here which bring us a little taste of happiness if only for a short time. And oh, my goodness your dad still watches Battle Rap with the TV volume still on 100 like you and him used to do. Evey day when I get home and turn on the TV, I must immediately turn the volume down. And yes, I still cannot understand why you guys watched Battle Raps and I still do not like it but that was yours and his thing. We hold on to the memories, some sad and some happy.

I remember you helping me look for us a new home and you would look up the homes and go drive by and facetime me when you arrived. You would say "mom you not gone like this house or neighborhood, because they have too many cars in the driveway" and we would laugh because we were being petty. Too bad the good times do not last forever. But at least I have the memories hid in my heart forever and ever.

Bri we finally found a house I think you would love it. We moved six months after you left us. And you knowing me know it was not an easy task. And yes, I got my porch, which is much bigger than I had in mind. I often sit on our huge porch and look on the other side and can imagine you sitting there talking to me with your bare feet (because you hardly ever wore shoes at home) and swinging your short legs and I smile, while we catchup on your off day of our weekly events. I hear your sweet high-pitched voice saying, "girl what happened" and I laugh or you say, "mom let me tell you".

Bri, I even let your dad and brother get a dog. We both know how I feel about animals in my house, but I finally gave in. Mainly because I am now outnumbered, and I tried to cheer them up because they do not say much but they miss you so much and it made them smile. But the funniest part is they let me name him trying to butter me up. I named him Onyx, which if I say so myself is a pretty cool name for a dog. I really think you would love him as much as they do. You know me, I like him a little bit, but he likes me a lot because, I always feed him, even though I am constantly asked not to give him food because he will not want to eat his dog food, but you know I don't listen sometimes.

Oh Bri, guess what? I started my Loc journey & I l love it so far. I also finally took that long-awaited trip to Arizona, that I always talked about going, which you thought I would never go. And to think I booked my flight and went on a vacation all by myself. You would be so proud of me. It was the most carefree peaceful trip I had ever taken. It was so beautiful there, and extremely hot. And I really enjoyed every moment of it. I wish you were here instead of me writing this in a letter to you. I have so much to say but cannot put it all in this letter, but let me continue before I forget.

Bri your favorite finally had a little favorite. If you were here, you would think he was yours. He is so cute and juicy. You would spoil him so bad. And for the baby shower I made sure to incorporate something red from you for him.

I miss you so very much. Bri you forever changed my life for the better. You were my first born arriving a whole three months early weighing in at only one pound and 10 ounces. You were a fighter than and I can without a doubt in my mind think that you fought to stay here but God had other plans.

I often wonder to myself do our loved ones become angels and watch over us. I'll know for sure one day. Some say when we get to heaven there are no family members and that loved ones are not angels. That part I am not sure of, but you are our angel.

I am so grateful to have had the task of being your mother. You helped me to grow up and taught me how to have unconditional love for someone. You made me so very proud of the hard-working independent young lady you had become. You never asked us for anything, because you were a responsible young lady. I often smile because I think I didn't do too bad at raising you. Even though you called me bougie, you had me beat. You would go into the store and fill your basket without ever looking at a single price tag unless, I asked you how much something cost, and you would shrug your shoulders and say you didn't know. I always laughed and thought that was funny. To me that was bougie something I could not do.

I am missing you and there is not a day that goes by that you are not thought of. I found some voicemails that were on my phone that I sent to my email to save. I saved them but have not listened to them yet. One day I can listen to them but just not right now. I do not know why I have not listened to the voicemails yet but knowing I have them gives me some comfort as well. You are forever engraved in our hearts, and we will forever love you and keep your memory alive! I love you, Bri. I'm ending this letter for now but never my love. Continue to rest well my Tootie Pop.

I love you forever and always.

Mom

Life Interrupted Reflection Questions

1. Has anyone or anything held you up from grieving?

2. How have you been able to process your grief?

3. Writing assignment:

4. Take a moment and journal your feelings and reflections at this time. Avoid censoring or critiquing your writing, just write what you feel and what comes. No one else will read it. It's only for your eyes only.

CHAPTER 4

Grief as a Family Unit

When a family grieves, each member wishes to take the grief away. I cannot count the times I wished I could take away the pain that her brother and father were feeling. It hurt me even to know they were hurting so much. I know it may sound strange, but I felt as though I could feel or was also carrying some of their pain as well. Then I had to realize this is a walk we all must take alone in order to cope with her death and began to heal.

I learned that people really don't have the appropriate words or phrases at times when people are grieving. They say well meaning things, but they are not helpful or comforting at the time.

I will never forget the day one of my friends made a very interesting statement, "I know you are angry with God," they insisted. "No, I am not," I replied quickly. Shock was left on their face. I was not angry at God at all. I needed Him now more than ever; her death drew me closer and closer to Him. It was because of God that I was able to face another day.

However, I did have questions, like "Why?" I did not understand how this could have happened and it was so sudden without a warning or even a chance to say goodbye.

It was not what any of us, not even my child expected when we awoke that Sunday morning. I remember thinking in my mind that not a single sole on earth wakes up and says today is the day I die.

My thought process was filled with countless questions early on in my grief, "Did my child know she was leaving this earth that very day?" "Was she in any pain?" "Was she ready or even prepared?" "Did she even have time to say a prayer?" Did she try to call out my name or scream for help?" "Did she know she was loved?" Why did her appointed time come so soon?"

A parent's joy and peace come from the positive impact their child makes on others. I know in my heart that my daughter's life made an indelible print on many people. There were key times when a friend, neighbor, colleague, or family member would share how they experienced my daughter, the stories were so beautiful and comforting. At times I found myself laughing and crying with gratitude.

Everyone deals with grief differently and they have their coping mechanisms, and for me I took a lot of time for myself to pray to my Savior Jesus, fast and worship and to think of all the memories we shared together.

When patient people would let me, I talked about her death often. I needed the release and l was always grateful for those who let me talk about her. That's part of the healing process and every griever needs unique people that would offer that gift to let them talk about their loved one. My prayer is that you who are reading this book, would find safe places and safe spaces and safe people that will make sacred room for you.

I thank God for the 23 years that He gave us with my daughter. There is not a day that goes by where she is not on my mind. I allow myself to feel what I need to feel in that moment when I think about my daughter. If I have to shed a couple of tears or laugh through the pain, I give myself permission to do so. You can do that too.

Grief for everyone is and will be a different walk as I have said before. Let no one and I mean not one single soul tell you how to grieve or how long to grieve. We have to grieve at our own pace and in our own way in our own time. I personally will not and do not put a time limit on grieving or healing for that matter. Why? Because everyone's experience will be a different walk through the process.

Also, because there is no right or wrong way to go about the grief or grieving process in general you will grieve in your own way. Let me say there is a wrong way to go about it when it's harmful to you. If your grief sends you to abuse drugs for relief, drinking alcohol, self-inflicting pain, dark isolation, perpetual spending, eating, and emotional bondage, then you may want to seek additional support (i.e., therapy, support groups, faith community). This is the wrong way to grieve and that is why you need safe spaces and safe people.

People don't know your story or what you have to go through behind closed doors in order to get up every single day and do this thing called life when you have to do it without that loved one being there that used to be there. People do not know how integrated the person was in your life and how much space they took up.

Life Interrupted Reflection Questions

1. What has been helpful on your journey of grief?

2. What inappropriate statement has been said or offered to you as a means of comfort?

3. When you reflect on your loss, what can you find to be thankful for?

CHAPTER 5

On The Other Side of Pain

When you lose someone, people have many questions for you when they see you have not lost your mind or your stability. I do not want anyone disillusioned about the process of grief or the pain that still lurks and emerges throughout your journey.

When you are living on the other side of pain, you still have to show up for life and do life as you once did before. After the family leave is over, after the PTO is fully spent, and the vacation days have been exhausted, you still have to show up and because you have resumed your normal duties does not mean everything is well.

I say living on the other side of pain because, there is still healing to be done as your life continues and you move forward the best way you can.

So, here is what you do. You walk in the reality that there is a big hole in your heart where your loved one possessed, and you accept by faith that God is filling that hole with his love, grace, mercy, kindness, strength, peace, power, and lovingkindness. God is present every step of the way. You are not alone.

You will feel fear and uncertainty when you take that bold step to rejoin life because your confidence and assurance has been shaken to the core. Death has a way of robbing you of everything you thought you knew for sure. Death teaches you to treasure each family member wholeheartedly every moment, every day, every way that you can. Nothing is for sure; nothing is guaranteed, and nothing is solid but the Solid rock of God on which I stand. He is the only guarantee in life and the only constant present help in times of trouble and tragedy. That is what Death has taught me. So, I hold on to Him on the other side of pain that much more.

It is also the process of knowing the pain is there, but you seem to somehow learn to get through each day until it lightens. Remember it's not time that heals all wounds, it's what you do with the time that heals all wounds. Praying, talking, counseling, and reflections help to heal and continues to help heal my deep loss.

Integration is a large part of healing. How do I integrate my loss with my present life. I don't deny it, I own it and it's a fact of life. I give myself permission and grace to embrace that truth. You learn to integrate your pain with your daily life and manage it with tools that you learn from the wisdom and science of others.

I want to share with you a poetic piece I value entitled "on the other side of pain."

Being on the other side of pain

Is the God-given ability to love again.

Yes, after a loss so deep

God promised you joy after you weep.

Being on the other side of pain there is still fear and tears.

But holding on to God's unchanging hands is your only cure.

On the other side of pain there is a bright hope; it makes it hard to understand how you are able to cope.

On the other side of pay you can even feel joy in the midst of it all, because His presence is righty there at every call.

Grief can't stop you or rob you from going on, Trust in His promises and He will make you strong.

Jesus wept when Lazarus died, but for all of us one day we too will rise.

My daughter is sleep only for a season; why she left so soon, I find no reason, but my hope is that we too will see each other again

And be able to praise our Savior and it will never end.

On the other side of pain there is His shalom and peace, I cannot explain how He lifts the burdens and allows the release.

On the other side of pain, there is gain as long as my faith remains in Jesus Name!

In a real practical way, living on the other side of pain for me is getting up each and every day grateful that I get to do it again and correct any mistakes I made the day before. I am not perfect but I try to be the best part of who I am each and every day I am allowed to be here.

The gift of God's Peace cannot be explained. It's a gift. That simple, and I receive it daily. I feel it even when things and situations occur that may not be peaceful, he sustains me in it.

I have also gained a strength that I was not aware that I even carry. Sometimes the peace and strength that I now carry is hard to embrace. The reason I find it hard to embrace sometimes is because I feel guilty sometimes, because I talk to others that have had loved ones to pass and they have not experienced peace or the strength I have, at least not yet. I have to release the guilt and trust God with their journey that He will give them peace as well.

I am called to remember the moment I kneeled down before God right in the mist of my tragedy and asked for peace and strength and He blessed me with both and for that I am so very grateful.

"So with you: Now is your time of grief, but I will see you again and you will rejoice, and no one will take away your joy."

JOHN 16:22

Life Interrupted Reflection Questions

1. What do you find on the other side of disappointment, grief, or loss?

2. Describe your life since your life interruption.

3. What have you learned most?

4. What has been the impact of your outlook?

5. Has your experience positioned you to help others?

CHAPTER 6

One Day At A Time

L ife is for the living because it does not stop when tragedies occur in our lives. The sun keeps rising and the moon keeps setting. The clock keeps ticking and the alarms continue to sound. Everything continues in the rhythmic motion set in order.

If I've learned anything and I have learned a lot, life will go on no matter what state we are in physically, emotionally, spiritually, or financially. Also, in order for me to carry on and thrive, I myself must take it one step at a time, one day at a time making sure life is not wasted. I value life now more than ever.

One thing that I have also kept in mind is that I will have what I say. It is vitally important to keep a sound mind and a positive mind on this journey. So, I have to continue to feed my spirit with positivity, the Word of God, healthy thoughts, prayer, fasting and meditation in order to continue to heal.

In the process of grieving even though you are hurting deeply, it is good to be nice to others and show them grace (kindness) even on the days you are feeling overwhelmed with grief. It will make a difference in how you are feeling. Responding negatively out of your grief will only build up a reservoir of guilt and sadness in you. Don't forget to show kindness to yourself.

What about the what ifs?

Out of all the tricky turns that grief can take you on, the road of "what ifs" is the most harmful. You will replay and replay the scenario over and over again in your mind, especially if you were within distance of your loved one before they passed and even if you were not remotely close.

- What if I stayed with her?

- What if I didn't go to sleep?

- What if I followed my first mind?

- What if I didn't feed them that meal?

- What if I didn't argue with them?

- What if I let them have their way?

- What if I had insisted on them staying home?

- What if I had driven faster to the doctor?

- What if I had changed my medical plan so they can get better care?

- What if we were happier?

- What if I had picked up the phone?

- What if I had made the event after all?

The "What ifs" will run over and over and over in your mind and run you crazy if you don't get off of that endless road.

I had to conclude that life and death are not in my hands but God's hands. God says in His word, there is an appointed time for every man and woman, boy and girl to die. This means no one dies out of order or without the watchful intending eyes of God. God is powerful enough if He wanted my daughter to still be here, COVID or any other threat could not have prevented her from leaving.

Somehow, someway I had to make peace with God's Sovereign will. My daughter was only destined to live 23 years just like Jesus was only destined to live 33 years on this earth. Somehow and someway in God's infinite wisdom, the time is already set from little infants, pediatric patients, early adults to senior citizens, what day they will meet their maker.

I would have loved many more years with her, but this is not the last stop!

Grief has a natural toil on your body, mind and spirit. It also has an impact on your interpersonal relationships with other children, your spouse, your co-workers and parents. It can make or break a marriage and friendship.

My humble advice is to be as open and as honest as possible with those important relationships in your life. Remain respectful, and by no means shift the blame on each other about the death of your loved one.

There are many things to fight on the grief journey. I had to fight that thing called guilt over and over again. For instance, I wondered why God let me live through Covid. They call it survivor's remorse. Then I had to fight guilt for being able to move forward with my life. I had to pray and know that God had prepared me for a time such as this (death).

During these times, I leaned on my community of support that surrounded me from my family, my pastor, and my spiritual sisters and brothers who kept me lifted in prayer.

One's ability to move forward in the midst of your grief can be shocking. Two weeks after my daughter's death, I went back to school to finish my degree. Some attempted to talk me out of it, but I knew I had to finish for me and my daughter. I also knew if I took time off, I would not finish. My inspiration was my daughter. When I got my last two degrees in May of 2022. I said "Bri I did it" that was a proud moment for me, because I know if she was here, she would be proud of me.

Don't forget about yourself

I take time out for me now without being preoccupied with what anyone else thinks or says. A wise man (my dad) once told me "Go while you can because there will be a time when you cannot go" So I often think of that saying and I go.

If you are not able to pick up and complete a goal, dream, or return to work as fast as you had hoped, have grace for yourself. Do not judge yourself. You will when it's your time.

There is a flood of emotions you will feel at any given moment when you are in a season of grief.

I personally have had times where I would go through anxiety. Anxiety was always triggered if I heard someone was sick or did not feel well. My mind would automatically go to my daughter's death. Instantly, I would be afraid the person would die. I would have to pray my way through it.

It's also a good idea to write or keep a journal. You can even write letters to the loved one that has passed on. It worked for me.

In the tough times I had to and to this day still seek God in the moment that I began to feel pain tugging at my heart. I pray and cry out to Him as much as I need to. That is where I find my center, my joy, and my peace. I can find myself sometimes crying and then I start to pray and soon my prayers began to turn to worship, and then I began to thank Him for the time I did have with my child.

What about the siblings

In grief literature when there are surviving siblings, they are often referred to as the invisible grievers because most of the attention is given to the grieving parents.

Please pay close attention to your children's needs because they can and will slip into despair and depression no matter their age.

Prepare yourself to have a real conversation or age-appropriate conversation with your child. Some hospitals and community programs have resources called "child life" that can assist the family in discussing death and its meaning with the surviving child in age-appropriate language. They can affirm and validate what they are feeling. Sometimes it is too hard for a grieving parent to have the conversation.

It is also important to look for changes in them that may let you as a parent when it may be time to seek clinical help for the child. Family therapy is very helpful and affirming. It brings healing in ways that seal the family as one unit and no one is ashamed at all to need the additional support. Even if one parent feels they are okay, being present for the other family member makes a world of difference.

Like a movie, people will watch you as you go through your grief to see how you handle your tragedies in life. I was often told how strong I was. That would irritate and frustrate me until one day, I recalled I did pray for God to give me His strength and His peace. So, it's, not so much that I am strong, but the Word says in my weakness, then He is Strong in me. So, I began to share with people that I can endure, because I kept my mind stayed on Him and He promised to keep me in perfect peace.

Life Interrupted Reflection Questions

1. How have you shown kindness to those in your life during your grief.

2. Take a moment and write down any what ifs that you pondered during your season of grief.

3. Did you struggle with guilt? How did you process it?

CHAPTER 7

Dos and Don'ts

Dos and Don'ts of Support Through the Grief Process

- Do be there as a support person: Support can be a number of things such as being there to give them comfort, being a listening ear, praying with them, holding their hand or just being in their presence are ways to show support.

- Don't ask questions right off like; What happened? How did they die? Were they sick? Where did they die? How old were they? (Please allow them to volunteer information about their loved one's death and if they do not, please do not ask, they will talk about details when they are ready).

- Do reach out to show your care by sending a card, flowers, calling them, dropping off a meal, offering to do a small chore (chores like running an errand, doing laundry, picking up medicine, ice, water etc.).

- Do let them know if they need to talk, they can reach out to you and really mean you are there if they need you.

- Don't say you will be there in their time of need and have no intentions of being there.

- Do let them grieve in their own way and listen.

- Don't interrupt a person that is grieving with comments like; they are in a better place, God needed another angel, everything happens for a reason, I know how you feel, you are so strong (this is the one I got a lot and at that moment you do not want to hear that remark).

- Do seek clinical help if you need it.

- Don't tell people you need to go see a therapist or a grief counselor right when they lose a loved one (I was told this right after my daughter's death by a random person that did not even know me that well and was taken back) First off this is not something to just ramble off. Again, I say everyone's experience with death is and will not be the same, you do not know if that is what they need.

- And most important never say to a person you are still grieving. Grief is a process and no one on earth can tell you how to grieve or how long to grieve.

- Do show support and be there if you are asked to help with funeral or memorial services.

- Don't give unsolicited advice or try to take over when you are asked to help with making any kind of arrangements for a loved one.

Also keep in mind that not everyone will experience death the same or deal with it in the same way. Death is a very painful traumatic emotional experience that you will have to figure out how to maneuver through in your own way.

CHAPTER 8

Strength From the Scriptures

Scriptures of Comfort, Healing, Peace and Suffering

"Blessed are those who mourn, for they will be comforted."
Matthew 5:4 (NIV)

"Blessed be God, even the Father of our Lord Jesus Christ, The Father of mercies, and God of all comfort; who comforteth us in all our tribulation, that we may be able to comfort them which are in any trouble, by the comfort wherewith we ourselves are comforted of God."
2 Corinthians 1:3-4(KJV)

"And God shall wipe away all tears from their eyes; and there shall be no more death, neither sorrow, nor crying, neither shall there be any more pain: for the former things are passed away."
Revelation21:4 (AMP)

"These things I have spoken unto you, that in me ye might have peace. In the world ye shall have tribulation: but be of good cheer; I have overcome the world."
John 16:33(KJV)

"Yea, though I walk through the valley of the shadow of death, I will fear no evil: for thou art with me; Thy rod and thy staff they comfort me"
PSALM 23:4(KJV)

"He heals the broken hearted, And binds up their wounds [healing their pain and comforting their sorrow]."
PSALMS 14:3(AMP)

"My soul dissolves because of grief; Renew and strengthen me according to [the promises of] Your word."
PSALMS119:28 (AMP)

"When thou passest through the waters, I will be thee; and through the rivers, they shall not overflow thee: when thou walkest through the fire, thou shalt not be burned; neither shall the flame kindle upon thee."
ISAIAH 43:2 (KJV)

"Not only so, but we also glory in our sufferings, because we know that suffering produces perseverance; perseverance, character; and character, hope."
ROMANS 5:3 (NIV)

"So do not fear, for I am with you; do not be dismayed, for I am your God. I will strengthen you and help you; I will uphold you with my righteous right hand."
ISAIAH 41:10 (NIV)

"Therefore encourage one another and build each other up, just as in fact you are doing."
1THESSALONIANS 5:11(NIV)

"Thou wilt keep him in perfect peace, whose mind is stayed on thee: because he trusteth in thee."
ISAIAH 26:3

Ways to keep a positive mindset:

- Focus on happy and positive thoughts

- Pray

- Meditate

- Read

- Write

- Track your day in a journal

- Exercise

- Volunteer

- Laugh

- Smile

- Do self-care

- Try new experiences

- Live a healthy lifestyle

- Surround yourself with positive people

- Do something nice for others

- Take breaks throughout your day

- Spend time with loved ones

- Socialize

- Take a trip

- Do daily affirmations

- Forgive yourself

- Believe you can do anything

- Let go of your past

- Remind yourself how blessed you are

- Reach out to others with a phone call (don't text)

- Rejuvenate

- Most of all relax, live, and enjoy life!

Don't wait till tomorrow, live life today, live and learn and keep on living and learning.

~Trina

ABOUT THE AUTHOR

Katrina Fisher-Geter

Katrina "Trina" Fisher-Geter lives in Tennessee with her family. She is an educator of 20 plus years. She is a graduate of Southwest Community College with an Associate of Applied Science and also a graduate of Liberty University with a Bachelor's in Business and Health Science. She is also a member of Sigma Chi Psi Sorority (Bridging The Social Gap). She loves to travel, shop, and read in her spare time. This is her first literary art. Her mission is to be a positive light through life interruptions and encourage others to get through the tough times in life.

– KATRINA FISHER-GETER –

www.ingramcontent.com/pod-product-compliance
Lightning Source LLC
Chambersburg PA
CBHW020336130626
46549CB00003B/1198